RANGER RICK'S BEST FRIENDS

HI, I'M RANGER RICK, the official conservation symbol for young members of the National Wildlife Federation, and leader of the Ranger Rick Nature Clubs. On behalf of all the animals in Deep Green Wood, welcome to our world of nature and wildlife.

THE BEAVER'S WAY

by Keith Hay

**Created and Produced by
The National Wildlife Federation
Washington, D. C.**

1 Trouble at Beaver Dam

by J.A. Brownridge

Chasing each other through the meadows, Ranger Rick and Cubby Bear charged down to Beaver Pond. The waters of their favorite swimming hole sparkled in the sun. Dragonflies and butterflies danced in the warm air above the pond's surface. Deer nibbled the fresh grass at the water's edge.

"Last one in's an old dinosaur!" Ollie Otter called, joining the race. He reached the bank first and dove in gracefully. The other animals followed as best they could, tumbling and splashing and laughing. No one was last!

"Well now, isn't this great?" Cubby said, lying on his back in the cool water while Mike Muskrat splashed him.

"And here comes the guy who's really responsible for the Deep Green Wood Swimming Pool," Rick said. "Hi there, Billy Beaver!"

"Well hi, gang," Billy said shyly, smiling with his big front teeth. "Nice day for a swim, isn't it?"

"I didn't know beavers ever took a day off," Ollie Otter said with a grin. "I thought eager beavers never stopped building dams and lodges."

"Don't kid him, Ollie," Rick said. "If he hadn't worked so hard on his dam, the stream wouldn't have been blocked

here—it would just be more marshland—and we'd have no swimming pool.''

"Hey, look at that black cloud, you guys!'' called Cubby Bear from the bank. Over the trees to the south great storm clouds had appeared. A tremendous flash of lightning from one of them almost knocked Cubby down, and a clap of thunder drowned out his words. The trees bent under a fierce wind. Great raindrops began to fall.

"Everyone back home to shelter!'' shouted Ranger Rick between thunder claps. "We'll meet back here whenever this storm is over. So long, Billy. Thanks again for the swim!''

And for days and nights it did rain. Hundreds of animals were homeless, their nests and burrows washed away in the flood. Billy Beaver's dam that had always seemed so solid was swept away the first night of the endless storm (which was, in fact, a hurricane). And for days after that the waters poured down, destroying the banks of the river, flooding and ruining the marshland.

Finally, it cleared and the Rangers gathered at headquarters where Rick was trying to organize a recovery team.

"We're all going to have to work

hard,'' said Rick when everyone was together. "First of all, let's go to Beaver Pond and see exactly how much damage has been done down there and what we might do about it.''

Ollie Otter was the first to arrive. And, because the weather had grown hot again, he leaped happily into the stream below where the pond had been. Almost as quickly as he had jumped in, he popped up to the surface with a sour look on his face. With a single motion, he threw a dead fish up on the bank at the feet of the watching Rangers.

"What's wrong?'' called Rick.

"The bottom is just filled with silt. The water is so full of sand and other stuff that you can't even see,'' replied Ollie angrily. "The water's so full of mud no fish could live in it.''

"This is even worse than I thought,'' said Rick anxiously. "We'd better see Billy Beaver and ask what we can do.''

But Billy Beaver was already busy getting new timbers for a new dam; he was chopping down trees far up river.

The other animals didn't know what to do; they gazed helplessly down at the ruined marshland. After the dam burst, the sides of the old pond and stream had been left unprotected; they were now scarred by eroded gullies where heavy rains of the last week had raced down unchecked into the valley below.

"First thing we've got to do,'' ordered Rick, "is clean up. You fellows good at digging, get busy and get up the dead fish, that old boot, and that old tire stuck in the mud. The rest of you, spread out and collect the trash around the pond.''

Cubby Bear turned quickly to start on his assigned job. But, without looking where he was going, he slipped on the mud, fell flat on his back, and slid slowly to the bottom of the bank. Try as he would, he couldn't get a foot planted in the mud to get back up the hill. Rick had to form all of the animals, who were laughing at the helpless bear, into a living chain. Finally they pulled him up the bank to safety.

"You'd better go upstream and wash off a little bit," said Rick. "Then come back and help us, but stay away from the edge of the pond."

It wasn't long before all the debris had been cleared away. Then Rick ordered the animals to get sticks and shrubs to put in the bank and stop the erosion until grass could grow. Meanwhile Billy could rebuild his dam and get the water back in Beaver Pond.

"I know it took you a long time to build the original dam and your house," Rick said to Billy, "but this time we'll all help you and see if we can't get it done before winter comes and many of you are left without homes."

Billy and his family had already begun to bring fresh-cut trees for the new dam. Other animals dragged the building materials over to the edge of the stream. And when enough stacks were piled together, Billy and his family began putting them in place, fastening them down and filling in the cracks with mud as only beavers can do.

After several days' hard work, things were beginning to improve. But it would be a long time before the pond was filled up and things were normal.

A weary group of animals finally gathered around Rick and Billy Beaver.

"We've done as much as we can for the time being," said Rick. "The rest is all up to you, Billy, Mike, and to the rest of the marsh dwellers. I hope you still have time to gather and store your winter supply of food. If you have any trouble, come and see us and we will try to help you through the winter."

"Thanks very much," replied Billy. "You have all done so much to help us. Many of us surely would have died if you hadn't—all because of that hurricane."

"That's right," answered Rick. "The storm helped us realize how much you beavers and other marsh dwellers do for us animals and for people, too. You build ponds and keep the river banks in shape. Maybe if we could get more people to read the pages of this book, they'd understand how important you are. Let's try it, and see if people appreciate beavers more by the time they meet us all again in the back pages."

Mr. Paddletail and his Family

Meet Mr. Paddletail, the beaver, chief of Mother Nature's corps of engineers. His way of life changes the look of our land. When he builds a dam to make his home, he can flood acres of ground. In the pond that forms, he builds his lodge and raises his family.

The beaver is an excellent swimmer. He can go as fast as six miles an hour under water. When he swims he makes his front feet into little fists and presses them against his chest. Or with his front feet he carries mud and stones.

When he swims on the surface, only his eyes, nose, and ears are above water. When he dives down and swims under water, he has special eyelids that protect his eyes yet let him see clearly. Flaps of skin seal off his nose and ears and keep the water out.

The beaver likes fresh water. It lets him swim to safety, helps him reach his food supply, and allows him to transport his building materials. The

A beaver steers with a built-in rudder. No wonder he's called Mr. Paddletail.

9

In the colorful days of fall, the beaver readies his dam and lodge, making them tight and snug against the winter's ice and snow.

beaver pond also provides homes for many kinds of wildlife. Ducks swim on it and build their nests on its shores. Fish swim in it. Moose, elk, and deer find it a favorite place for food and a cool drink.

Mr. Paddletail is a wise master builder. In the safety of the middle of the pond that forms behind his dam, he builds his lodge of wood and mud. It has several doors, a living room, and even a chimney. Sound like your house?

The living room is a hollow cave nibbled out of the large mound of sticks and branches. Its floor is covered with dry bark chewed into long,

A lodge covered with snow makes a safe shelter for the beaver family.

soft strings. The walls are made tight against the winter's cold by packing them with mud. But the top of the lodge is left free of mud so that air can flow in and out—as if out of a chimney. On cold days "smoke" seems to come out of the rooftop. (It is really the beavers' body heat rising into the winter air.)

The beaver family is called a "colony," and usually consists of a mother and father, youngsters over a year old, and those born in the spring. Sometimes an uncle or aunt or a grandparent will live with the family and share the work. An average beaver weighs between 40 and 60 pounds and measures about four feet from his nose to the tip of his paddletail.

Winter seems to make prisoners of the beaver family by sealing the pond and the lodge with a thick layer of ice and snow. But snuggled together in their warm fur coats, they stay in their lodge secure from such enemies as a bear, bobcat, or wolf. When the beaver gets hungry, he simply dives out one of the holes he's made and swims under the ice to his winter food cache of stored branches. He selects a branch and returns to his den to nibble.

Mr. Paddletail eats his food just as

you eat corn on the cob. He sits up, holds the stick in his forepaws, turns it, and chews off the bark, the main part of his diet. After feeding he simply shoves the branch outside, and in the spring the peeled branches are added to the dam.

When spring comes, the beaver's life changes. He must check the dam and repair winter's damage. In May Mrs. Paddletail gives birth to two to five babies, called kits. Father and the older brothers and sisters leave the lodge so that for the first two weeks mother can raise her young in private. The newborn kits grow fast on their mother's rich milk.

They have tiny flat tails and sharp front teeth. After several weeks mother teaches them to eat water plants and tender twigs.

If you are very quiet as you stand near the pond, you can often hear the kits whimpering inside the lodge. They sound like little puppies crying for food.

Swimming is easy for the kits. Their soft furry coats are waterproof and help them float like a cork. Their back feet are webbed like a duck's. The flat tail is used to help swim in water and balance on land.

Mr. and Mrs. Paddletail keep a sharp eye on the kits. If danger is

A beaver emerges from the lodge through the underwater door *(right)*. The cut-away drawing at left shows two hungry beavers bringing branches home for chomping. A third beaver swims beneath the ice to the food supply stored on the bottom of the pond.

to nibble on tender twigs and leaves.

near, they slap the water with their flat tails, sounding a warning that sends the kits to the safety of the lodge. Danger can come from the sky with hawks and owls who want a dinner of young beaver. On land, they must watch for coyotes, bears, and bobcats.

As the sun begins to set, Mr. Paddletail leaves his lodge. He works, eats, and plays during the night while we are asleep. The first rays of sun may send him back to his lodge to rest.

During the summer he is a "lazy" beaver. He spends his time loafing, eating, and just getting fat. During the long winter his layer of stored fat will help keep him warm.

The tender inner bark of trees such as poplar, willow, and birch is among his favorite foods. But in the summertime he loves to munch on sedges and water lillies. He will not eat meat.

The beaver's way is to be neat; he spends hours combing his beautiful fur coat. He uses a special claw on his hind legs to comb his fur. Body oil from oil glands at the base of the tail is combed through the fur to keep it soft and waterproof. The long outer "guard" hairs protect the thick underfur that keeps him warm and dry. When he swims his skin never gets wet.

When Mr. Paddletail senses the first signs of winter in the air, he changes quickly from a "lazy" beaver to an "eager" beaver. From early evening to late morning he is busy gathering food and repairing his lodge and dam. His tools are his four powerful, chisel-like front teeth, paws with flexible fingers, and his strong flat tail, which he uses to prop himself upright while cutting a tree. His front teeth never stop growing. They are kept short and sharp by gnawing. He can cut down a 4-inch-thick tree in 15 minutes. A

Mother beaver pushes a five-day-old kit out of the water (left). Older and larger kits (right) return to a lodge after a swim and have a snack. Tired mother beaver rolls over on her back. How do you like the inside of their house?

family of beavers often cuts more than 1000 trees each year. Beavers have no control over which way a tree will fall. They have even been killed by their own cut trees falling on them.

As Mr. Paddletail cuts nearby trees, he must go farther and farther from his lodge to find more trees for food and dam-building materials. He

The beaver uses his sharp teeth to cut down trees, even big ones, and then builds a strong and sturdy dam.

is clumsy on land and wants to stay close to the safety of water. So he seeks to build new dams and make larger ponds. Canals must then be built from the edge of the ponds to other stands of trees. The trees will be cut into small pieces and floated through the canals.

Logs, sticks, and stones are carefully placed by Mr. Paddletail in the stream so as to form a U-shaped dam across it. The bottom of the U points downstream. Each new log is wedged into place. Then small sticks, mud, and stones are placed around it. Mud and stones are scooped up from the stream bed and placed on the upstream side of the dam. Soon the shallow pond forms. More sticks, more stones, and more mud are wedged into place. As the dam grows higher, the pond grows larger. The dam is now a strong, tangled mass that will last for years if kept in good repair.

The dams Mr. Paddletail and his ancestors have built help prevent erosion and flooding during the wet periods. In time the old ponds fill with soil and form beaver meadows. Farmers use these areas for crops and grazing land. Mr. Paddletail is one of our most valuable soil and water conservationists.

3 "Eager Beavers" . . . that aren't really Beavers

OTTER

"What's going on around here?"

Mr. Otter rises to his full height. His bright eyes shine and his black nose sniffs as he explores the outside world. To him it holds few dangers and many chances for the games he likes to play.

Mr. Otter's particularly good at games in the water. He is the champion swimmer of all the fur bearers, fast and graceful. But watch how he swims—he doesn't always paddle with his feet. Sometimes, he bends or flexes his body up and down in a rippling motion. Try it the next time you're in a swimming pool.

Whiskers twitching, the otter sits up on his hind legs, supported by his tail.

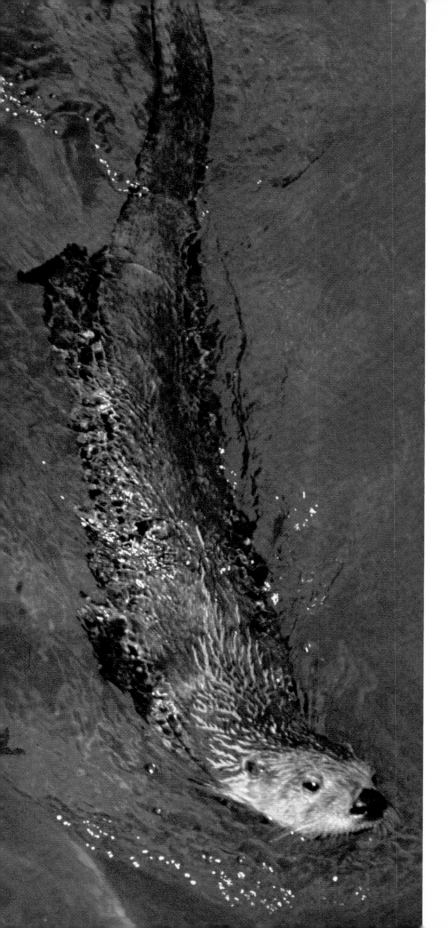

About half the size of the beaver, his streamlined body easily distinguishes him from Mr. Paddletail. But like the beaver, waterproof fur and layers of fat keep him warm and dry. He, too, seals his nose and ears when he dives.

The otter has lightning-like reflexes and can easily catch a fish. Unlike the

above. In this safe home, one to five kits are born in April or May.

Some morning by the riverbank you might hear strange chattering and splashing. The quiet is broken by the otter family as they take turns sliding down the slippery mud bank on their stomachs into the water. The chuckles and whistles and "hahs" sound a lot like your friends at the neighborhood swimming pool. In winter, otters make long slides in snowbanks. Do you think that—if you had a fur coat—they'd let you join them?

The otter, a fast and easy swimmer, can even catch fish. Clamping a bass in his jaws, he takes it ashore to eat.

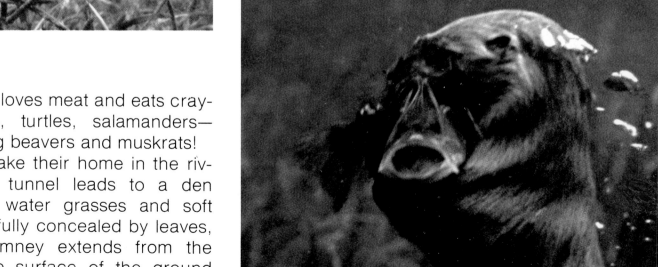

beaver, he loves meat and eats crayfish, frogs, turtles, salamanders—even young beavers and muskrats! Otters make their home in the riverbank. A tunnel leads to a den lined with water grasses and soft bark. Carefully concealed by leaves, an air chimney extends from the roof to the surface of the ground

MUSKRAT

Do you think you might ever see a lady muskrat floating along on a raft enjoying a cattail for lunch? Perhaps, if you are lucky, you really might. This is because the female muskrat builds floating platforms of reeds and cattails where she may dine and look out for predators.

Muskrats live wherever there are streams, ponds, or marshes. As you watch them swim, you will notice they push the water back with their large hind feet and hold their front feet under the chin. The long, thin, hairless tail wiggles back and forth like a rubber rudder, while the soft, thick fur keeps them afloat and dry.

The muskrat lodges you see are piled-up marsh grasses, twigs, and cattails held together with mud plaster. These rest on the bottom of the shallow pond. Homes may also be tunneled in riverbanks. If you could cut them open (as the artist has in

Waterproof coat, rudder tail, and strong feet suit the muskrat's marshy world.

The muskrat builds a house of marsh grass and cattails. In a severe winter he may eat the inner walls of his lodge.

the drawing below) you'd see that each lodge, like the beaver's, has an underwater entrance leading to a cozy, grass-lined nest above water level. In summer the muskrats build simple grass nests.

Sometimes muskrats depend upon the beaver for water, food, and shelter. They chew a tunnel into an unused portion of a beaver's lodge and build a nest. The beavers never mind these free-loading intruders. Both kinds of families seem to live happily in their separate apartments.

Although muskrats prefer to eat marsh plants, they also like lots of other food—insects, crawfish, frogs, and fishes. They are also clever

enough to get along even when the pond freezes and food's scarce. They go hunting under the ice. But how do they breathe when they can't come up for air? As they swim they make bubbles that form air pockets just under the ice. When they need air they nose up into these pockets for their oxygen.

Muskrats must always be on the alert for predators: hawks, owls, snapping turtles, large fish, otters, weasels, raccoons—and their most deadly enemy, the mink. No wonder they build such long tunnels and clever hideaways. You may be sure that when the lady muskrat goes rafting she keeps her eyes open!

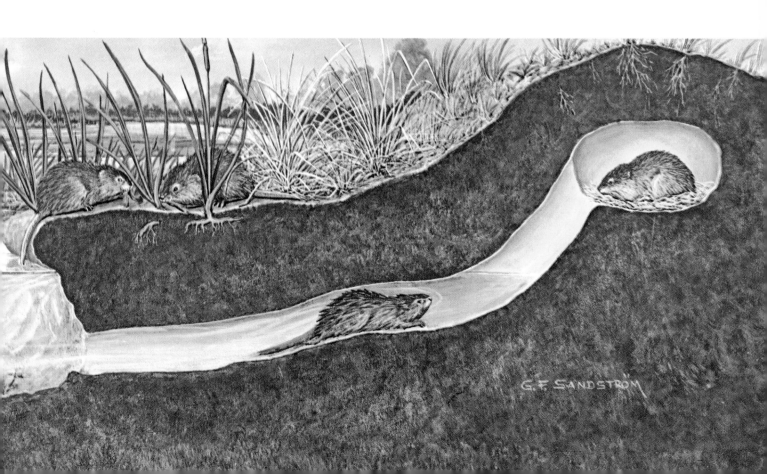

G.F. SANDSTROM

by J.A. Brownridge

Dawn had not yet broken over Deep Green Wood. Most of the animals were sound asleep, curled up comfortably in their nests or burrows. Only the hoot of an owl and the scurrying of night creatures disturbed the silence and sent quick shadows across the moonlit landscape.

Suddenly the sound of hurrying feet came down the trail. A voice called breathlessly in front of Ranger Rick's den in the great tree.

"Psst, Rick! This is Mollie Muskrat. Please come quickly. There's a mystery down at Beaver Meadow, and we marsh animals need your help to solve it."

"Mystery, Mollie?" Rick asked sleepily. "It seemed peaceful and normal when I was down there yesterday."

"That was before the strangers arrived, Rick," Mollie pleaded. "And I mean *real* strangers . . . strangers like you'd never believe!"

"You mean you're just worried about some animals you've never met before?" asked Ollie Otter who had been waked up by their talking.

"No, Ollie, of course not. These strangers I've never seen before anywhere—or even heard about in school. And . . . let me tell you the worst thing." She beckoned Ollie and Rick to come closer and listen carefully. "The worst thing is that these strangers are pretending to be beavers or otters or *muskrats*!"

"That does sound pretty strange," Rick agreed. "Do you think they're from another part of the world?"

"Or another planet?" asked Cubby Bear who had joined them.

"We'd better look into this," Rick decided, scampering down the tree and putting his hat on.

"But wait a minute, Rick," said Ollie. "If these strange animals are really *strange,* they may be enemies from some place. We'd better watch out."

"And we'd better have a good plan," added Cubby. "We'll *surround* them."

"Now don't get so excited, boys," Mollie said. "I didn't mean to start an

4 Ranger Rick and the Muskrat Scramble

army; I just came to ask Rick's help."

"That's O.K., Mollie," Rick assured her. "The more rangers you can get to help you with a problem, the better. Come on, you guys—let's go quietly. I'll lead the way."

So while the night wind blew a few clouds across the face of the moon, the rangers walked cautiously along the path to Beaver Meadow. "Shhh," Cubby said every few steps; but he seemed to be the one making the most noise.

When they reached the meadow, Mollie Muskrat motioned them over to a corner of the pond they'd never seen before. From the deep water grew big reeds and tall grasses too tough for muskrats to eat. But as the rangers stood quietly in the dim light they could hear—chomp, chomp, chomp—*somebody* eating.

"We've got to wait until daybreak before we can really see them," Mollie whispered fearfully.

"All right, Mollie," Rick said. "Don't worry: we'll stay right here until it's light.

Then if we find anything bad, I'll go get Ranger Tom."

That thought made them all feel better. Cubby settled himself down for a short snooze. Rick and Ollie tried to stay awake until dawn, but they could feel their eyes get heavier whenever the moon went behind the clouds.

Mollie kept watching but was too nervous to concentrate. In the first light of the new day, she didn't notice that two big eyes were watching *her.*

The strange animal started to come nearer. The sudden noise woke up Rick as Mollie let out a single yelp.

"Hi!" the strange animal said. It had great big whiskers and four large, orange front teeth just like a beaver's. "I'm Nina Nutria. Who are——?"

But before she could complete the question, Cubby and Ollie and Mollie were tumbling over themselves, heading for the deep woods as fast as their legs could carry them. Only Rick stayed behind to introduce himself and hear Nina's interesting story.

Later Rick gathered the Rangers around him to tell them how Nina had originally come to the United States.

"A number of years ago," he said, "some people who trap and sell furs decided to import a new kind of fur-bearing animal from South America. Then they started breeding them here. The animals were really called coypus, but because they looked a lot like other marsh animals, they also were called *nutria* (which is Spanish for otter). The only trouble with the trappers' plan was that nutria pelts were too hard to prepare for the market—so they stopped hunting them."

"That was lucky for the nutria," Ollie chuckled quietly.

many times before when people have imported animals from far away. The new arrivals soon multiply so fast that they become pests and must be controlled some way.

"But don't be discouraged, Mollie. I know help will soon come. I know that the Rangers who read this book will better understand the balance of nature and will make sure that management of wildlife is done only with advice from trained biologists."

With a reassuring wave, Rick ran off to take Mollie's problem to Ranger Tom.

"Yes, but not for the muskrats," Rick went on. He explained that nutria have no natural enemies in North America. They eat nearly the same things muskrats eat and, since they are no longer hunted, they breed very rapidly and eat up many of the biggest and best reed islands in lakes. That makes it difficult for the muskrats.

"Oh, dear. I knew they meant trouble," Mollie said. "Too much competition for food will mean a lot of us will starve or get sick."

"Yes, that is too bad," Rick said soberly. "It's another case of people tampering with nature without knowing what they're doing. I'll go back and tell Ranger Tom about it.

"Ranger Tom will get the Fish and Wildlife people to start some controls and bring our wildlife back into balance with its habitat. This has happened

WHEN YOU SEE A BEAVER . . .

Watch him comb and dress his fur with the split nails of his webbed hind foot. He combs his fur to take out tangles and to keep it smooth.

Look closely at his bright orange enamel front teeth. The rear portion is dentine which wears down faster than the front. Thus the teeth have a chisel-edged shape. The beaver likes to chew. Since his four front teeth are constantly growing, he *must* chew to keep them short.

Admire the beaver's large, flattened, paddle-shaped tail. Close up you can see its leathery scales are six-sided figures, or hexagons. See if your friends guess that this picture shows the tail of a beaver!

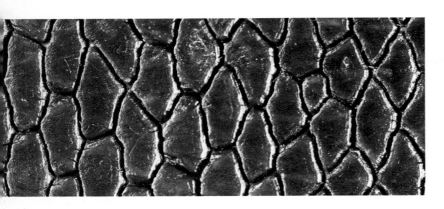

CREDITS

Leonard Lee Rue IV beaver cover; Jack Swedberg and Carl Scott pages 2-3, 11 top; Thase Daniel 8-9, 22; C. Allan Morgan 10, 11 bottom, 21; Jen and Des Bartlett, Bruce Coleman Inc. 13, 14, 15, 16, 17; Leonard Lee Rue III 18, 19 top, 24-25, 27, 32 top and right; Robert Dunne 19 bottom; Russ Kinne, Photo Researchers Inc. 20; Elgin Ciampi 22-23; George H. Harrison 26; Victor B. Scheffer 32 left; G. C. Kelley back cover. Artwork Chet Reneson 12; G. F. Sandström 26-27.

NATIONAL WILDLIFE FEDERATION

Thomas L. Kimball	*Executive Vice President*
J. A. Brownridge	*Administrative Vice President*
James D. Davis	*Book Development*

Staff for This Book

EDITOR	Russell Bourne
ASSOCIATE EDITOR	Bonnie S. Lawrence
ART DIRECTOR	Donna M. Sterman
ART ASSISTANT	Ellen Robling
RANGER RICK ADVENTURES	J. A. Brownridge
	Robert Brownridge
RANGER RICK ART	Lorin Thompson
COPY EDITOR	Virginia R. Rapport
PRODUCTION AND PRINTING	Jim DeCrevel
	Mel M. Baughman, Jr.
CONSULTANT	Edwin Gould, Ph.D.
	The Johns Hopkins University

OUR OBJECTIVES

To encourage the intelligent management of the life-sustaining resources of the earth—its productive soil, its essential water sources, its protective forests and plantlife, and its dependent wildlife—and to promote and encourage the knowledge and appreciation of these resources, their interrelationship and wise use, without which there can be little hope for a continuing abundant life.